zendoodle coloring

Baby Animals

Other great books in the series

zendoodle coloring

zendoodle coloring

Baby Animals

Adorable Critters to Color and Display

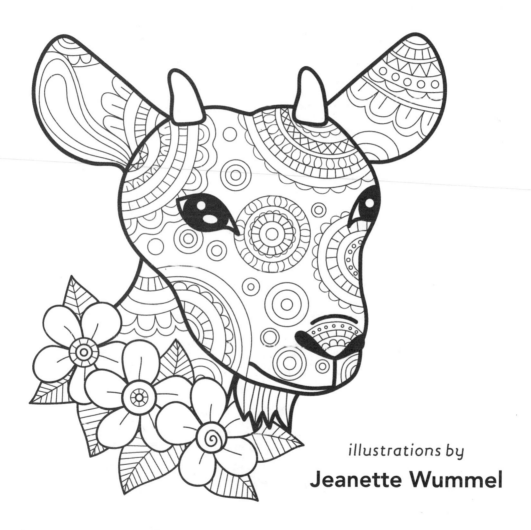

illustrations by
Jeanette Wummel

ST. MARTIN'S GRIFFIN

NEW YORK

www.stmartins.com

ISBN 978-1-250-10902-6 (trade paperback)

Our books may be purchased in bulk for promotional, educational, or business use.
Please contact your local bookseller or the Macmillan Corporate and Premium
Sales Department at 1-800-221-7945, extension 5442, or by e-mail
at MacmillanSpecialMarkets@macmillan.com.

First Edition: September 2016

10 9 8 7 6 5 4 3 2 1

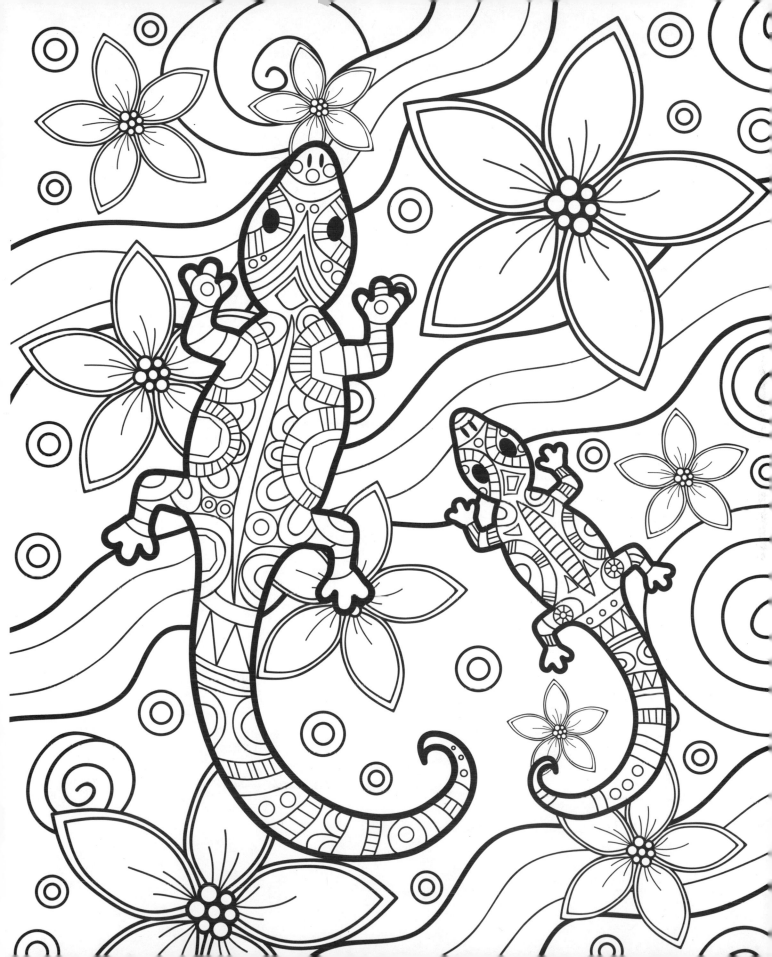